*The Baby's Not Settling*

# The Baby's Not
# Settling

A COLLECTION
OF POEMS BY

## Terry McHugh

SHAMROCK LODGE PRESS

This book is designed and typeset by
Once Upon Design, Drogheda, and
published by
Shamrock Lodge Press
Shamrock Lodge
Ballymakenny Road, Drogheda, Ireland

ISBN 978-0-9564023-0-1

Printed in England by
MPG Books, Bodmin, Cornwall

# FOREWORD

Terry McHugh's habit of listening out for the moment when a poem strikes home has borne fruit with the publication of his first collection of poems, *The Baby's Not Settling*. Over the years I have grown used to Terry calling by my house to read a new poem to me, a poem hastily written down on a sheet of paper and later copied into a hardback notebook. Gradually the collection gathered pace.

The photographs complement his poems very well, especially those of people or places which Terry mentions in his poems: his grandmother's house, his elderly friend Tom Maguire, the Boyne river, Beaulieu Pond and, further away, Ypres, an infamous battlefield of the First World War.

Something that stands out in this collection is Terry's respect for the elderly, his fondness for visiting them every week and listening to what they have to say. The poems tell us that he feels at peace in the company of these old friends. In several poems about nursing homes he expresses an empathy for their physical and mental deterioration.

The reader of this collection is left with a sense of life turning full circle. The poems range from descriptions of Terry's young years, often spent at Shamrock Lodge, the home of his grandparents, to poems about growing up and having his own family, to his feelings of protection towards his newly born grand-daughter, Caragh.

There are also darker poems in this collection and reading them we come to realize that school was not a happy place for the poet. However his grandmother provided some comfort and a poem describes him much further on in his life as 'ruddered by knowing family'.

Terry loves to walk deep into the countryside in the early morning and these walks have provided him with a harvest of poems and ideas. *The Baby's Not Settling* is a welcome addition to the rich store of literature by Drogheda writers. I wish him well with this collection.

SUSAN CONNOLLY

# INTRODUCTION

My first emotion as I write these lines is one of humility.

To merely put together a few thoughts as an opener to a project that must have required discipline, application and the searching of the depths of recollection is kind of superficial in comparison to this completed work.

The Author's quest in search of his own self can be elusive, deceptive and an unfaithful mistress as far as the memory is concerned. However, the pursuit can be rich with stories, memories and anecdotes.

The honour felt in writing this epistle is commensurate with my respect for the Author. He is a collection of contradictions that would have frightened Freud as he has evolved from the flame-haired Viking warrior of the schoolyard (ask any of his peers!), to the cultured musical and loving family man and friend of today.

Finally, the most pleasing aspect of this work is that, despite the morally barren soil of State, Church and School, this sapling tale of honesty and how it was, has struggled, survived and now surfaced.

'Full many a gem of the purest ray serene
the dark unfathomed caves of ocean bear'. (Gray's Elegy)

Here's your gem, read on and prosper ...

TOMMY AYRES
School Reporter (retired)

Cheers!

# CONTENTS

# PREFACE

As I endeavour to put pen to paper in my writing room, the merciless hand of exhaustion is somewhat weighing me down. This book has been quite a journey. The logistics of a project like this can certainly test one's mettle.

I was a big reading fan as a child and Saturday evenings were spent going around my friends' houses swapping annuals and comics, before settling into my Grandmother's bed for hours of reading and sweets. I clearly remember the first book I ever read. I owe Robin Hood and his Merry Men a great debt for transporting me onto the pages of a wonderful journey.

My love of poetry was nurtured in first class at primary school. The very first poem I read was a very simple pastoral gem:

> 'If I had a house, I'd live on a hill,
> I'd reap and sow and plant and till,
> I'd grow good oats and I'd grow good hay
> and in my little fields I'd lay.'
> (Thanks Kerry)

I was smitten from then on.

Words have a power all of their own and of course they last forever.

Some of you might be puzzled by the title of this book. The answer can be found in the very last poem. It has been quite a literary odyssey all these years.

The very act of writing this collection of poems has had the cathartic effect of settling the errant baby a little – sixty years later.

# ACKNOWLEDGEMENTS

This is the humbling part of the book.

Susan Connolly has been my main-stay and wonderful friend throughout this project.
Words fail me.

Kevin Brogan has used his computing skills and provided some classic photogr[a]
along the way. What a man!
Words fail me.

Jimmy Weldon has been with me from the start; I thank him for his cover pho[to]
and friendship.
Words fail me.

Caroline Kavanagh for typing out the original draft and being such a pal.
Words fail me.

Michael Holohan for his wise words and for sharing his great creativity.
Words fail me.

Jim Fuller for his expert advice and patience.
Words fail me.

Martin Healy of Four Courts Press for his unfailing assistance and camaraderie.
Words fail me.

My brothers and sisters, thank you, especially my Goddaughter and sister Louis[e]
– what a beautiful person.
Words fail me.

Finally,

To my wife Patricia, daughters Kerry, Clodagh, Erin and Claire, my son Shane
– thanks for being there!
Words fail me.

*To the beautiful spirits of Shamrock Lodge, who look down on me as I pass by every morning and who permeate this book from start to finish.*

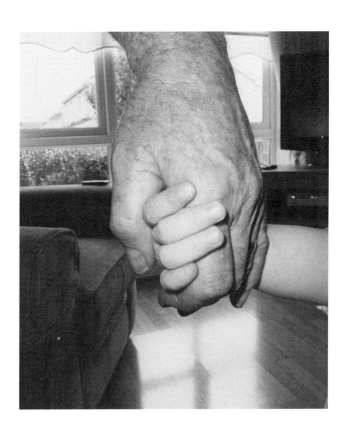

# FOR CARAGH

You won't remember clasping my finger
from two generations ago,
when you were just one day old,
or how we exchanged our very first glance:
how that magical moment made emotions dance.
I knew then that I had to write this memory
for you to hold, before life turns cold.
I am fifty-six and you are preciously new.
Calming the waters for you as I pass along the way,
waiting to greet you along the tree-lined glade.
You'll be big enough then, to hold my hand and talk
excitedly of when we had it made,
when I was fifty-six and
you were just one day old.

# WHEN I GROW UP

When I grow up I want
to be a man because
I'd have money for Mar bars
and give the cat my all-bran.
Walking down the road swinging
freedom across my shoulder;
I'd shout and talk back.
Happiness is, to be older.
I could stay out all night
and come home in the light of day;
never again have to fight,
and against dozy haystacks I'd lay.

# NO REASONING

Could science put the white into snowdrops,
or prize open the daffodil blooms?
Could it make dahlias dance their windy tune,
or force the orchids into ruin?

Could science conform the black sheep
or freeze the heated heart?
Could it stop genetics' prodigal parts
or locate love's golden key?

Could logic cradle a dying enemy
or make a lone last stand?
Could it self-inflict bleeding wounds
or bring ecstasy from breakfast sounds?

# FOR KAZUKO

When the morning sun

opens Irish eyes,

a new dawn beckons as

Japan welcomes the onset of night.

Different strings of

the same samisen

where music is the oil

for life's lantern.

# JUST LIKE JAPAN

The church steeple looks across
the Irish countryside
like Buddha on his throne,
casting forth a silent voice.

The trees look to heaven
as they do in Japan.
Cattle shelter under
their leafy gaze.
The time is now.

# FATHER

Father was a victim of his time:
where expression of
affection was weakness,
love could only mime.

A lonely childhood walked
through life beside him.
Driven to success by traumatic times,
a grim toll continually stalked.

A heart attack at forty-six:
dead at fifty-five.
He knows how much I miss him.
I always have.

# SULLIVAN'S FIELDS

Sullivan's fields and I were best friends:
the railway bridge was my theatre
where one-man armies won every war
and Jack Frost danced through invisible doors.

# THE SCATTERING FEATHERS

The feathers left the pillow as if
resurrected on the geese.
Children playing innocent games
froze at the sound of angry footsteps,
slim cane, frenzied user.
Terror and rebellion grew.
The walls remember these nights.
Memory written into young pores.
Darkness wins.

# THE SILENT DOOR

Like its former inhabitants
the green door lies still.
Only the flowers remember
with a colourful celebration.
There were glad times here,
the bees still take their fill.
Better any times than no times.
Noise then, now there is none.

The door still commands a sad dignity:
please notice as you pass by.

# EMOTION

Detachment's cold hug
was the only mourner at
the funeral,
and he only came to gloat.

# THE EAGLE'S SON

If I were the son of an eagle

I would glide with the confidence

of indifference,

display more grace than

the chattering seagull

and rejoice in the

forest's aromatic scents.


My parents would be engulfed

with pride

as I float on the cushioning wind,

bear witness to the

departing tide

and contemplate the chicken's

white skin.

# THE REST HOME

The old ladies at the other table

vie with each other in the talking stakes.

This table is sadly silent.

Three elderly men sit staring

towards oblivion.

Nothing to say or see.

Time means bed, food and fear.

The sign on the wall reads:

'This is Friday the 1st of August.

It's a damp and humid day.'

The family visit when they get time.

There's plenty of that here.

# ENTWINED LIVES

Mother and son live out of one life
for the price of two.
She nurtures her only child
when suddenly the
man brings the old lady her shawl.

She falls again – the ambulance is called.
Lying surrendered on a stretcher
she whispers to her man-child:
'I shall never darken this hall again.'

The call comes – Mother is breathing death.
He arrives as she's being wheeled into
the dying room.
Priest, nurse, family
by the bedside.
A life in a flash –
Mother dies.

# TWO MEN IN WHEELCHAIRS

Walking down the corridor
of the nursing home
I saw them by the long
window in their wheelchairs,
silently staring across the night,
not unlike nuns at prayer.

I stood there watching them
drift to another time.
Legs could walk,
tears could cry,
friends were forever
and they were pilgrims.

# FOR SALE

The weeds on the boreen
have no one to greet.
The hedges on either side
reach out in solidarity.
No tracks in the muck since
the hearse drove away.
Wildflowers bow in empathy
around the gate, and
only the mice can manage
the death dance.

The opportunist ivy
envelops walls and windows.
Plaintive cries from the past
bring tears streaming down kitchen
walls in damp disguise.

Cold wind whistles around the
broken hall windows,
as damaged hinges torture a once
welcoming front door.

# THE VISTA

I am looking and I can see
a blackthorn bush stubborn
against the breeze.
A lone robin sits gaily
on the gate
basking in the morning mist
as a marauding cat
prepares to seal its fate.

I am looking and I can see
the sun shine through the rain.
Small children dance in puddles
laughing happily.

I am looking and I can see
my grandmother stoking the
dying embers on St Stephen's Day,
a vision of Christmas gone.

# ODE TO A CLASSROOM

*'The times were bad and we were in bad hands.*
*There was nothing to be done only record'.*
(Thomas Kinsella)

Brother Ryan's classroom stood

apart from the rest.

Never leaving the eyes.

Youth lost in an

overflowing ink-well.

He smelt like a Christian Brother.

Chalk and sweat, pervasive and smothering.


The Primary Exam results in his hand.

First place brings esteem

only to be stripped of clothes and dignity.

Gratification over, he sends

his student home with his prize:

a blue fountain pen.

# SOUNDS

The sizzle of the sausage,
the crashing of the waves,
the hissing of the cat,
magic notes from the stave.

The cawing of the crow,
the whistling of the wind,
the frost frozen furnace,
the tenuous ties that bind.

# THE BROTHER

I didn't see him, but I
knew he was in the rest-house.
I'm the last of us at home.
Visitors told him how I was.
I'd see him about twice a year.

He died last evening –
it doesn't matter.
His presence is always here.

# SERVICING THE BOILER

The boiler-house door hasn't
been opened since last year.
Diverse insect families
gaze disdainfully out from
under the burner,
become animated, agitated,
frustrated at
my unwelcome intrusion.
Their noisy silence fascinates.
The boiler-house door closes,
delivering sanctuary
for another year.

# GRANDMOTHER'S HOUSE

Playing marbles on the old stone floor,
waiting for the kettle to boil
on the blackened hob.
The wonderful clinking of her delph
as she laid the table
are secure sounds that have
journeyed through life
alongside me.

I still feel her warm touch,
still reach for her outstretched hand.
I see her trying to light the fire
on St Stephen's Day.

# BYRON

Byron the patrician laced in silver,

polished by greedy genius.

Described Keats' 'Piss the bed poetry'.

Betrayed by his own eloquence.

Hailstones of history melt for Keats.

# THE CHILD AND THE TREE

The boy loves the tree,

its hanging branches hugged from above.

The trunk listens

because imagination can't lie.

The fox looks across,

a rat looks up,

the squirrel looks down.

The tree takes no notice.

It's sharing a confidence

with a special friend.

# THE HEALING

The young man visited his grandfather:
they spoke about relationships.
He explained that his own father loved
and admired the old man very much,
despite an adversarial past.
The grandfather nodded sadly and
hugged his grandson.
The young man quietly
left the graveside.

# THE PHOTOGRAPH

Time cannot change the
colour of the hair.
Taut skin won't loosen
on the bones.
Searching eyes will never dim,
remaining cool as sacred stones.

# A STAIRCASE
## (PIPERSTOWN HOUSE)

I am the stairs.

Families walk on my steps.

Strangers admire me

in spite of my age.

I'm part of a palatial pile,

a mahogany slave

torn from my roots

to join two floors.

Whatever they call me,

I come from the earth's core.

I am a tree.

I am a tree.

# PHEASANT

The young pheasant gloried in
the open spaces,
fragrant honeysuckle a
mere backdrop in an
embarrassment of beauty.

The three dogs would growl
scarily at him, but he
was free and they weren't.
The humans seemed very nice.
Summer was great that year
and the young pheasant
played gleefully in
the huge rhododendron bushes.

He wished that sleep hadn't
been invented because it
calmed his ecstasy.

He was now growing into
a really beautiful bird.
The stone out-houses in
the courtyard were a haven
for many creatures.
The owl assumed
the mantle of
nocturnal look-out.

One glorious day followed another,
like different blooms taking
over the sea of colour
when their counterparts faded.

Autumn came in its stockinged feet.
The leaves waved goodbye to
the trees, but not before
basking in a celestial colour change.
There was warmth in nestling together.

Then, in early November, just as he was
gliding from the bushes,
the humans shot him dead.

# DUNLOE

A horse sets his sights on the Gap:
the cow's eyes follow.
Their gaze travels on the moonlight
before resting on the gate.

Tranquility lays its bed
across these fields.
A heart beats slower.
The guitar sounds sweeter.
Darkness falls.

# DANTE AND ME

I drifted with Dante in the Duomo.

The portrait read 'Divine Comedy'.

His words were mine,

my eyes were his.

We shall engage again.

# FIFTY

My father lived to be fifty-five.

Time's getting short.

October is fitting for reaching fifty.

The evergreen sneers at the prostrate leaf.

Naked trees bend like ballet dancers

in the winter wind.

Tranquility arrives exhausted,

having travelled the years:

fifty sorrows for

fifty joys.

# CHRISTMAS

The rampant fire lit up her
daunting drawing room,
heralding in Christmas Eve.
Curious, the old ash tree
peered in the window with a
snowy weight on faltering shoulders,
sighs of envy from her boughs.
Dancing shadows scanned the rafters,
bringing cobwebs and marauding mice
into passing prominence.
Logs stacked against the chimney
eagerly awaited their moment
in the light.
The night wind created a comforting
chorus against draughty window-frames
and latched up doors.

Jeanie, the old Cocker Spaniel, lay on the hearth.

I sat on Grandfather's knee listening

to stolen stories that came to life

in the yellow flames.

Crimson berried holly and ivy

adorned the old picture frames.

Santy knew about

Nellie's room behind the wallpaper

where all the bad children went,

but never in December.

I marvelled at the oil-lamp

as it flickered magically,

and the Christ child smiled

at our birthday preparations.

# FLORINTINA'S EYES

I see a lost world in her eyes,
the back of life laid bare.
Rescued from hell by love and care
saved everything but Florintina's eyes.

*Romania, May 2003*

# NICORESTI
## (A VILLAGE IN ROMANIA)

Dirt road in the dark,

pony's eyes lit by the moon.

Fox hushes his prey

until the rider passes,

rushing back to ruin.

# THE WEDDING

The wedding is over.

Bouquets wilt on gravesides.

The happy couple fly far away.

Father Tom returns to his empty house.

Families wonder at the

cruelty of time.

# BACK TO THE SCENE

I came back today to my old school.
As I walked through each room
furtive angst dammed the ducts.
I was moulded here to
see the world as a threatening place.

Brother Murphy sank his adult
fist into the side of my head
when I was ten years old.
Defiance revived me as I
picked myself up from the
cold concrete yard
and unleashed ten years of venom
on Murphy.

DUBLIN AND BELFAST RAILWAY,—VIADUCT ACROSS THE BOYNE, NEAR DROGHEDA.

# THE BOYNE

The river of myth and legend,
from erudite salmon to battles royal.
The perfectly arched viaduct watches
the water on its way to Newgrange,
a holy place where darkness
is eclipsed by light.
Medieval Drogheda is the child
of the Boyne where low lanes
and high lanes look towards
the Backstrand.
Brú na Bóinne sends aurora
skimming waves to the sea,
where the sky bids farewell
to the land,
and worlds are set free.

# THIRTEENTH OF APRIL 1969

Not long from an English sojourn,

met at a soirée in Dundalk.

She was water for thirst

solace to solicitude,

meat for bones,

silence for talk.

# TWO SEASONS

What blossoms the Spring could send
for Summer to decipher.
Morning dew would moisten
the new grass and
prepare the day
for wondrous things.

Feathered babies grow and sing,
then fly with abandon from
where the glades would ring
with the sounds of Godly
composers and perfect cadence.
Tiny apples look towards
motherly fruition.

The summer dresses the trees
and concocts the woodbine scent;
grants affirmation to flowery weeds,
then waits for it all to end.

# THE GHOST TREES

Light and snow are in league
with the trees.
Closer to heaven than
the church can see.
A white path hides the
footprints of the forever child
as he dances with the branches
so meek and wild.

Time enjoys the amnesia
that is peace.
The life-force shares empathy
with fallen leaves.
Hell has no sanctuary here,
everything to love,
nothing to fear.

# TWENTY-FOUR
# CHRISTMAS CARDS

Twenty-four Christmas cards

on proud display by her bed;

a fraction of her love

now being returned.

Each one slowly read – then re-read.

Her spirit strong, in

a body tired and worn.


With Marcella I could dispense

with false facades.

A salty woman of the land

where work was long and hard.

Her presence like an open hand.


Our weekly chats and her soft embrace:

treasures I carry along the way;

December draws the lines of her face.

Twenty-four Christmas cards, joyfully have their say.

# THE HIGHEST POINT

I'm crawling around this attic:
the rats and spiders are emphatic,
they don't take kindly to men
who invade their inner den –
a bit like Rangers and Celtic.

The lady of the house hasn't been here?
Then she doesn't know real fear.
I have droppings in my finger nails
and stuck to my knees.
Gay abandon is the haven where
a rat merrily pees.
He's made his point –
and points are very near.

# IN MEMORY OF JOHN B

When all the bishops' croziers
go for firewood, and
cardinals' hats dance on the
heads of clowns;
when Rome flounders
from where it stood,
your stories will still abound.
When Listowel leaves the Kingdom
and parish priests become redeemers;
when the sword is greater than the pen,
you'll remain a literary dreamer.
When rejection slips turn to gold
and drunks to strong willed men;
when hearty turf fires turn us cold,
you and I will meet again.

# LULLABY FOR A CHILD

Ah, little bamshin,
go to dream,
the fairies are waiting
by the old mill stream.
Ready to sail
in the cradle canoe,
along barely aggrieved water
of a silken shady hue.

The water-hens and otters
will guide your way,
passing ghost trees and castles
along fairy mounds of clay.
When the child spirit waves
as you sail by his home,
sing for him this lullaby,
my grandmother's heavenly song.

# SHAMROCK LODGE

The window shutters remember him
being carried in when he was a week old.
Clanging clocks recall trying in vain
to drown his cries.
Ornate chimney-pots remember
the wood smoke and the noise
of children and fires.
The old staircase recalls his grandparents,
jaded footsteps keeping time
with tired lives.
Holes in the stone floor remember
marble-playing children
now lost to the shadows.
Guardian trees recall rustling
an errant baby to sleep.
The summer-house ruin
remembers secrets they shared.
The old avenue recalls generations.
Warm kindness of Grandmother remembers
the short journey into his soul.

# THE BUTTERCUP FIELD

Birds sing among

the buttercups on the

hottest day of the year.

Tractor tracks flatten delicate

yellow petals as they

breathe in the sun.

Flies look for something

to suck up to while

silent feathers pick them off.

A young spirit

prances among the colours,

kicking the prickly thistles.

Broken eggshells lie

beneath the rejuvenated hedges.

Youth, wild as the flowers,

jumps through the badger gap

into infinity.

# ESSEX FARM CEMETERY, YPRES

He died a soldier, aged fifteen,

not long from picking blackberries.

Did his father get the bad news

when his day was nearly done,

or his mother from the chapel pew?

His short life over – been and gone.

# CHRISTMAS TRUCE 1914, YPRES, BELGIUM

Shaky candles shone bright,

lighting the German front line.

A soft voice danced across

the frosty no-man's-land.

'Stille Nacht – Heilige Nacht'

warmed the bloody sand

where young men pined for Christmas,

locked in the love of home.


'Silent Night – Holy Night'

harmonized the front line.

Enemies embraced,

candles burned white;

peaceful moments before death.

# YPRES

Join our tour,

see more graveyards,

maybe notice a cross

with a familiar name.

Some of them even contain bards

who might write –

'What price fame?'

# WHAT I WON'T REMEMBER WHEN DEMENTIA CALLS

I won't remember sitting in the pram
being scared of the teddy-bear;
or my first day in school
when tear ducts found
a ready dam.
I won't remember Brother Rockett
twisting the skin off my nose
when I didn't conform to
his mordant commands,
or being beaten, and warned
that left-handed children go to hell.
I won't remember poetry or prose
or the stories that I wrote and read;
or the teacher in Fourth Class
who checked my homework while
his sweaty hands surveyed soft genital flesh.

I won't remember being punched to the ground

by Brother Murphy when I was ten

before replying with an alphabet of expletives;

or the paedophile Brother Ryan presenting

my First Prize with malign intent.

I won't remember the remedial warmth

of my beloved grandmother in

the wonderful space of her old farmhouse.

I won't remember the horror

of my fourteenth February

that travels with me still;

or being envious of small birds as they

flew away from cats and penury.

# BEAULIEU POND

The bird symphony guided
my way to the water's edge.
A gentle breeze goaded
the reluctant ripples.
Families of swans congregated
to share my supply of bread,
as spirits from the deep
created aquatic dimples.

Crunching footsteps on the leaves
betrayed my presence to furtive animal eyes.
Wide open spaces
gave way to the overflowing water
of father time and tide.
Here, solitude can have its say.

# THE FALLEN GHOST TREE

You were the keeper of the backwoods.
Inspired by your silent strength
I reached beyond the visible.
Broad branches sheltered those within
as demon winds grew strong.

Loyal roots ached in empathy as
you fell back amongst your own.
Saplings whine against the wind
for a fallen icon.

# WINTER IN A BOY'S WORLD

The old house was the theatre
where he built his dreams.
Jigsaws of ice on the inside
of the bedroom window
wove winter magic.

Breaking the ice in the cattle trough,
greeted by cows clouding him
in their warm breath,
he waited for day to unfurl.

Skating down the ice-slide,
watched by his invalid grandfather,
enveloped him in a loving glow;
if only they could slide together.

# THE MAGUIRES

I love to see the old thatched roof
across the meadow,
hide-and-seek pheasants in hedges
and noisy water-hens flapping by the lake.

My memory smiles at simple men of the clay
as they chatter with whistling winds.
The patient evening that waits all day
for the red sunset.

Chimney smoke in the breeze speaks
of rain or sun and
cattle always know the way.
The harvest is won.
Innocent times for original days.

# IN MEMORY OF TOM

Monday, Friday and Sunday
were my 'Tom' nights.
The guest chair my throne
surrounded by cats.
Tales of how life was
or should be
told with an innocence that
floated through the air
like an infant's cry.

I was at peace there.
Mice danced in the attic
to the radio céili as
the envious wind looked in
through the crack in the door.

He's gone now, and the little
cottage is green with damp.
His beloved clocks have stopped.

# THE CHRISTMAS CARD

Christmas was made for happiness, not loneliness,

but my family are all dead and gone.

I'm too tired and frail to put up the tree.

I just wish I had somebody to hug, especially today.

Is that a noise in the hall?

A Christmas card waits – an answer to a prayer.

# THE STONE OF ARAN

The sea and sky were one as
we travelled on the boat to Inisheer.
Fishermen around the Cliffs of Moher
waved us on.
The island beach beckoned us
to cool our hot feet in its soothing water,
clearer than a glassless window.

Jutting out from the furtive sand
was a mysterious grey stone
with a perfect hole drilled
through it by the ocean sorcerers.
I rescued it from its watery grave.
I made the short walk to the island cemetery.
The chapel ruins looked mournfully
across the ocean waves as
weather beaten headstones stood
like stone soldiers against the elements.

# DREAMS

Sleep brings us before birth
and after life.
It conjures both oasis and desert,
makes way for angels and devils,
provides solace from pain.
Brings the dead to life
to effect posthumous reconciliation.

# THE HAPPY PLACE

At six years old he sought solace
in Granny's warm understanding words.
'No need to worry anymore,' she said.
'Tomorrow I'll take you to the
happy place where sweet boxes never empty,
hands are raised only in love
and we'll both live blissfully ever after.'

She followed that revelation by tousling
his red hair and drawing him
into her loving embrace.
From that moment on
those words, 'The Happy Place' would be
a banner across his soul.

Why had he not heard of this sanctuary
before now?

That night he slept the sleep of
the sweet dreamer.
After school the next day
he ran up the old tree-lined driveway.
He had secretly packed
some clothes into his school-bag.
'Are you ready to go?'
He could barely contain his joy.
'Go where?' his granny asked.
'To "The Happy Place", of course,'
he said, a little impatiently.
The old lady heaved one of
her familiar sighs before she
broke the bad news.

'It was just a little fairy story
I told you to contain your tears,'
she whispered softly.
He stood there in rigid dejection.

'We were going to be together
forever and ever,' he cried.
He ran across the yard
to the old summer-house ruin,
where he buried his traumas
behind the ivy clad stones.

# DID YOU SEE?

Did you see me when I was young?
A day seemed like a year
in the surreal art of growing up.
My father and I were highly-strung;
I listened to orders, but could never hear.

Did you see me when I was a teenager?
A rebel in a minefield laced
with the explosion of experience.
Not ready for the insidious dangers
of a race to oblivion.

Do you see me now I'm growing old?
The fire still burning,
dampened by what might have been.
Still unable to embrace the fold,
ruddered by knowing family.

# ST LAWRENCE'S GATE

The evening sun shines on
this thirteenth-century Barbican.
Spirits from the ancient St Lawrence's Priory
gather to sing silent hymns.
Ever-changing streets lead
into the ageless citadel that
stands tall against modernity
and exalts in its own place.

# A FACE IN THE CHOIR

At the first rehearsal he

knew that it wouldn't last.

The conductor knew his music,

but not men.

Like a classroom from the past,

rebellion settled in.

Gave it every chance – in vain,

Free spirit – speak out – a loner again.

# THE WILD GOOSE LODGE

The sprawling tree hangs
its branches across this
ruin of deathly screams.
Ivy and gorse conceal
what remains of stone walls.

Eight pleading souls burnt here
in a flaming hell,
while ribbon men laughed
their lives away.
A five-month-old baby
welded to his dying mother's arms.

The merciless wind batters
invisible rooms and scorns
at the naked thatched roof.

The quarter moon stands guard
over the weed strewn hall
listening for marauding hooves
and the voice of a
five-month-old spirit.

# FOUR THIRTY-FIVE, AUGUST DAWN

He said the headache was unbearable.

At least it wasn't his heart.

I started the car,

drove him to the hospital,

helped him in,

closest we've ever been.

I laid him gently on the bed,

sat with Mam in the next room,

two hour wait – two lifetimes;

told to contact family.

The time passed in dreams;

at four thirty-five, August dawn,

a nurse came in,

'I'm very sorry,' she whispered.

I cleared my head.

Never a right time

to share death.

# CORMAC

Don't go yet – I like talking to you;

I've terrible backache – I can't eat.

My lips are cracking with a desert dryness.

Eighty-eight years old now;

you're my only regular visitor.

Thirty-five years in Australia,

great place for a black sheep

although I was mother's favourite.

Don't go yet – I like talking to you.

What's your name again?

God! I'm sorry.

I can't smoke as much any more,

the horses don't win in my head like they used to.

What day is it?

Don't go yet – I like talking to you.

# FIVE LIVES

Saturday, Saturday, Friday, Monday and Tuesday;

Fifteenth, twenty-third, ninth, thirteenth and twenty-first;

dates sown into the psyche.

New lives to calm a torrid mind;

crystal hearts to fill with nurture.

Innocence to love and be loved;

tiny hands to hold, just like gold.

Fresh minds, not fooled by false eyes.

So vital to have a hero,

an umbrella in their rain.

A loyal memory at the end.

# FOR THE LOSS OF MY MOTHER

I saw my mother in a dream.

She'd been dead for a year.

Her clothes had happy seams.

I called after her,

she didn't hear.

I ran up to her,

'Mam, I thought you were gone.'

She turned round in a blur.

'Oh Terry' – her words melted

into a heavenly embrace

as the dreamy sun shone.

# THE ELECTRIC MOON

When the life long battle
with the world is over
and grudges are consumed
by the wet clay;
when the manuscript is not
judged by the cover,
love will still light the moon
at the resting of the day.

# THE TEST RESULTS

They were both summoned
to meet the oncologist.
Looking for body language,
The Last Post played across
the doctor's eyes.
'You've got cancer,' he said.
'We will do our best for you.'

He felt the tears well up:
she didn't look the same.
Everything changed in a sentence.
She deserved more happiness.
They held hands for the first
time since the early days.

His past danced before him
on the way to the car.
He wondered should he tell the children
as they passed the cemetery
on the way home.

# FORTY YEARS AGO

It happened last night – forty years ago.
Frosty February – Gate Cinema – The V.I.P.s –
ran away from home at fourteen years old.

Ten past eleven – the film ends.
Stomach churning begins.
Parental anger – beaten home – didn't cry.
Nobody there to save him.
Nothing worse.
His fear dies.

# THE SUMMER-HOUSE

I revelled in that special magic
reserved for children, when
playing in the ruins
of my grandmother's summer-house.
Made a secret bet with the ivy
that I would grow faster and stronger.
The ivy just rustled in answer.

When dusk fell, the call
to come home ricocheted
off the gable wall before
finding unwelcoming ears.
Trying in vain to avoid marauding nettles
I made my way across the field.
Before going in, I cast an
envious glance through the
fast fading light and
bid goodnight to the summer-house.

# SUNDAY MORNING

Early on a Sunday morning
a lone church spire babysits
the sleeping town.
Barking dogs wake the cursing wino,
making him gather his lives
and move on.

# THE BABY'S NOT SETTLING

She pushed and heaved – then
their second child was born.
All week in the hospital
he wouldn't stop crying.
She could hear the nurse:
'the baby's not settling.'
Those words rang in her ears.

Back home in her parents' farmhouse
she placed him in the furthest room
to escape the endless whimpers.

His grandparents were within earshot.
Granny couldn't bear to hear
a child in distress.

She crept over to the cot, and
carried her grandson
back to her bed where cries
were replaced by gurgles – and peace.

'Ah, little bamshin, go to dream,
the fairies are waiting by
the old mill stream.'

Her warm arms and soft lullaby
nestled in the baby's heart.